Animals with Super Powers

Shape-Shifting Animals

by Natalie Lunis

Consultants:
Christine Huffard, Cephalopod Biologist
Mark W. Moffett, Natural Museum of History

BEARPORT
PUBLISHING

New York, New York

Credits

Cover, © Sylvian Cordier/Biosphoto/FLPA, © Michael Durham/Minden Pictures/Corbis, and © Robert Eastman/ Shutterstock; Title Page, © Sylvian Cordier/Biosphoto/FLPA; 4TL, © Norbert Wu/Science Faction/Corbis; 4TR, © Robert Eastman/Shutterstock; 4BR, © iStockphoto/Thinkstock; 5T, © Aquapix/Shutterstock; 5B, © S. J. Kraseman/Peter Arnold/Getty Images; 6, © Aquapix/Shutterstock; 6–7, © Stubblefield Photography/Shutterstock; 7T, © Ethan Daniels/ Shutterstock; 8, © Michael Stubblefield/Alamy; 9T, © Ethan Daniels/Alamy; 9B, © Seapics.com; 10, © Peter Wirtz/ F1 Digitale Bildagentur GmbH/Alamy; 10–11, © motorman611/Public Domain; 11BL, © Liz Tuttle/Public Domain; 12, © Image Quest Marine; 13, © Steven Hunt/Photographers Choice/Getty Images; 14, © John Canclosi/Alamy; 15C, © Shawn Hanraham/Public Domain; 15, © Photoshot/Alamy; 16, © Peter Orr Photography/Getty Images; 17, © Ken Griffiths/NHPA/Photoshot; 18, © Michael Durham/Minden Pictures/Corbis; 19, © Peter Oxford/Minden Pictures/Getty Images; 20, © Andreas Mauricio Henao Quintero/flickr; 21T, © Brisbane Insects and Spiders; 21, © Auscape/ardea.com; 22T, © iStockphoto/Thinkstock; 22C, © Eric Isselee/Shutterstock; 22B, © Fotografos/Shutterstock; 23, © Eric Isselee/ Shutterstock.

Publisher: Kenn Goin
Editorial Director: Adam Siegel
Creative Director: Spencer Brinker
Design: Dawn Beard Creative
Photo Researcher: Brown Bear Books Ltd

Library of Congress Cataloging-in-Publication Data

Lunis, Natalie.
  Shape-shifting animals / by Natalie Lunis.
    pages cm. — (Animals with super powers)
  Includes bibliographical references and index.
  ISBN 978-1-62724-079-6 (library binding) — ISBN 1-62724-079-9 (library binding)
  1. Animal defenses—Juvenile literature. I. Title.
  QL759.L86 2014
  591.47—dc23

                          2013029546

For more information, write to Bearport Publishing Company, Inc., 45 West 21st Street, Suite 3B, New York, New York 10010. Printed in the United States of America.

10 9 8 7 6 5 4 3 2 1

Contents

Shape-Shifters

For hundreds of years, people have told stories about creatures that can change their shapes. For example, there are tales of vampires who turn into bats and humans who become werewolves. Does shape-shifting ever happen in real life, though? Are there any creatures that have the power to **transform** themselves into something else?

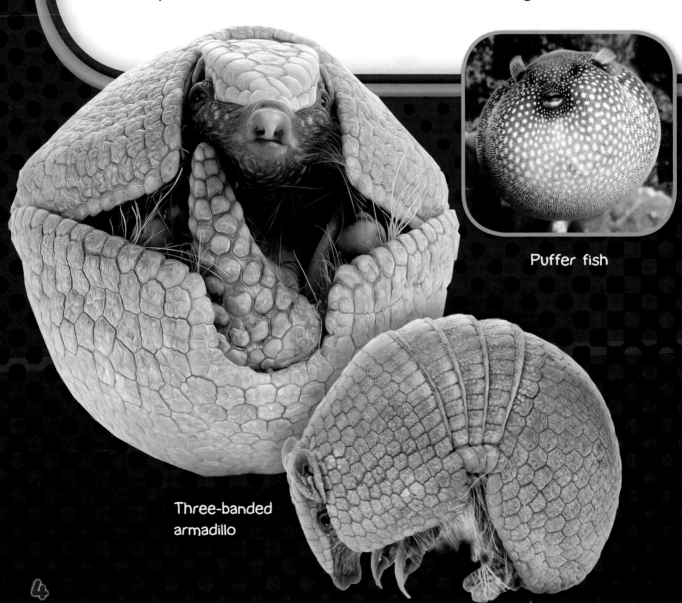

Puffer fish

Three-banded
armadillo

In fact, such animals do exist—and you'll meet eight of them in this book. Among them are a sea creature that can pretend to be a rock, a caterpillar that can rise up like a snake that is about to strike, and a fish that can blow itself up into a big spiky ball. These animals may all take on very different shapes, but they do have one thing in common. They use their shape-shifting abilities to scare off, escape from, or appear less tasty to their enemies. In other words, they use their special powers to survive.

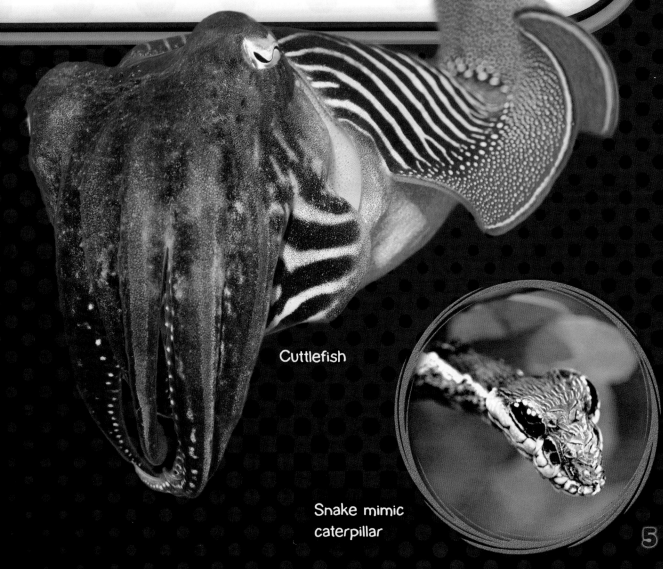

Cuttlefish

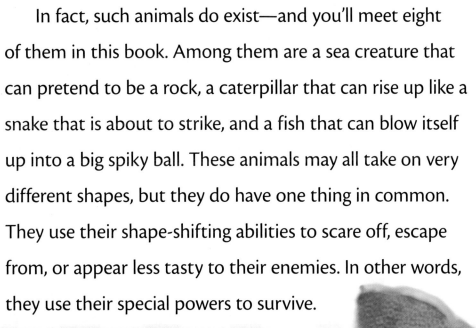

Snake mimic
caterpillar

Cuttlefish

A cuttlefish isn't really a fish. Instead, this creature with eight arms and two long **tentacles** is a relative of the **octopus** and the **squid**. A cuttlefish isn't a plant or a rock either—but it can change its shape to look like either one!

Cuttlefish need a good way to hide from hungry fish and other **predators**. After all, these undersea creatures have soft bodies and no shell to protect them. Luckily, their ability to quickly change both their color and their shape lets them blend right in to the background. In less than a second, they can go from being a tasty-looking dish to being just another part of the scenery.

There are more than 100 species, or kinds, of cuttlefish. They live in warm ocean waters near Africa, Asia, Australia, and Europe.

Cuttlefish can make their
skin bumpy or spiky when
they take on the shape of
underwater plants or objects.

After changing the way it
looks, a cuttlefish can hold
its new shape for hours.

Mimic Octopus

For a long time, scientists have known that octopuses can squeeze their soft, rubbery bodies into very small hiding places. It wasn't until 1998, however, that they discovered a special trick that one kind of octopus uses to stay safe from enemies. This octopus—known as the **mimic** octopus—puts on a **disguise**. How? It changes the shape of its body in order to look like other animals.

For example, the mimic octopus can gather all its arms together to make itself look like a **poisonous** leaf-shaped fish called the zebra sole. Or, by spreading its arms out in different ways, it can pose as a poisonous lionfish or sea snake. As long as the mimic is passing itself off as one of these fierce creatures, it doesn't need to worry as much about being attacked or eaten.

Mimic octopuses live in shallow, sandy parts of warm seas near Southeast Asia.

The mimic octopus also changes color when it puts on its disguises.

This mimic octopus has made itself look like a zebra sole lying on the ocean floor.

zebra sole

Zebra soles spend much of their time lying still on the sand at the bottom of the sea.

9

Blanket Octopus

Some people call it Batman. Others call it the Caped Crusader—and it's easy to see why. With a huge cape-like flap of skin trailing from its body, this octopus looks like an underwater superhero.

The strange animal's more common name is the blanket octopus. However, the flap of skin that spreads out behind its head is neither a blanket nor a cape. Instead, it is **webbing** that is attached to the front four of the octopus's eight arms. When the eight-armed creature feels threatened by a large fish or other predator, it **unfurls** the webbing. Most of the time, the change in size and shape works very well. The enemy leaves the octopus alone since it seems much too large and powerful to defeat.

Blanket octopuses live in warm waters in the Atlantic Ocean and the Mediterranean Sea.

Blanket octopuses
showing their webbing

Female blanket octopuses can be up to 6.6 feet (2 m) long. Males are much smaller—only a few inches (cm) long—and do not have cape-like webbing.

Puffer Fish

Most of the time, a puffer fish looks like an ordinary fish. It has a small mouth, a tube-shaped body, and a tail. In moments of danger, however, it changes in a not-so-ordinary way.

When the puffer fish meets up with a predator, such as a shark or other large fish, it quickly starts swallowing water. It can take up to 35 gulps in 14 seconds. Soon, it is twice its normal size and the shape of a blown-up balloon. It is also covered with **spikes** that pop out as its skin stretches. Not surprisingly, hungry enemies find the puffed-up fish hard to swallow—or even bite. They swim away in order to look for something they can truly sink their teeth into.

There are about 120 species of puffer fish. Most are a few inches (cm) long, but some are more than three feet (1 m) long.

This shape-shifter is known by many other names, including balloon fish, blowfish, bubble fish, and globefish.

Most puffer fish live in the warm waters of tropical oceans.

Snake Mimic Caterpillar

A caterpillar's soft, boneless body is a meaty treat for birds and other animals. To protect itself from these predators, one kind of caterpillar—known as the snake mimic caterpillar—uses a very surprising trick.

Most of the time, the snake mimic caterpillar simply blends in with the twigs and trunks of the trees it crawls on. If a bird comes too close, however, the little creature quickly changes its appearance. To do so, it drops down from a twig, hanging on by only its back legs. Then it puffs out its front end into a triangle shape that looks like a snake's head. After that, it lifts its brand-new "head" to show two spots that look like a pair of big, scary eyes. What comes next is no surprise. The caterpillar's enemy quickly backs off.

Snake mimic caterpillars live in forests in Mexico and Central America.

Every kind of caterpillar is the young, worm-like form, or **larva**, of a butterfly or moth. The snake mimic caterpillar is the larva of a brownish-gray moth that is known as a sphinx moth.

This is the moth that a snake mimic caterpillar grows into.

A snake mimic caterpillar is about five inches (12.7 cm) long.

15

Frilled Lizard

Usually, a **frill** is a decoration, such as a bow or ruffle. It makes those who wear it look fancier and prettier. However, the opposite is true for one kind of lizard that lives in Australia. Its frill is meant to make it look tougher and scarier!

A frilled lizard spends most of its time in a tree. While it is there, the lizard stays safely hidden. The large flap on its neck lies flat against its body. Sometimes, however, when the **reptile** goes down to the ground to look for food, it meets up with a snake, fox, or other enemy. That's when its frill fans out to full size. Shocked, the enemy freezes in place. Meanwhile, the lizard makes a quick getaway by running back up a tree—and out of reach.

When the frilled lizard is in a relaxed mood, it's not easy to see the lizard's neck flaps. They just flop down loosely.

A frilled lizard is two to three feet (.6 m to .9 m) long. Its frill measures up to one foot (.3 m) across when it is fully fanned out.

Frilled lizards come down to the ground in order to look for insects, spiders, and other small animals to eat. They also lay eggs on the ground.

Three-Banded Armadillo

For some shape-shifters, bigger is better—especially when they are faced with an enemy. For others, becoming smaller and rounder is a super way to stay safe.

The three-banded armadillo is a small **mammal** that lives in South America. Its body is covered by a hard, bony shell that acts as **armor**. Because the bands that connect different parts of the shell can bend and stretch, the armadillo can roll itself into a ball when it feels threatened. Then its head, legs, tail, and belly are safely tucked in. Once it has changed its shape, predators, such as alligators and jaguars, have a hard time trying to bite or grab the roly-poly creature.

Three-banded armadillos are about ten inches (25.4 cm) long. They eat mostly ants and termites.

There are other kinds of armadillos besides three-banded armadillos. All of them have armored bodies, but none of them can roll themselves into a ball.

19

Bird-Dropping Spider

Bird droppings look disgusting—and not at all like something a bird or other animal would want to eat. That's good news for the bird-dropping spider. This little eight-legged creature is able to survive in forests in Australia because it looks just like the stuff it was named after.

Even though its black-and-white body looks like a pile of poop, this sneaky spider doesn't take any chances. During the day, while it is resting, it tucks its legs in so that they do not show. Now it really has the color and shape of something a bird left behind—and that other animals should leave alone.

When it is walking, a bird-dropping spider looks pretty much like any other spider.

bird dropping

Bird-dropping spiders hunt at night— while the birds and wasps that hunt them are resting. Hunting at night also makes it hard for some of the spiders' other predators to see them.

With its legs tucked in by its sides, the spider fools its enemies by looking like a bird dropping stuck to a twig.

More About
Shape-Shifting Animals

Cuttlefish

A cuttlefish disguises itself as a plant or rock not only to hide from enemies but also to sneak up on the fish, crabs, and other animals that it hunts and eats.

Most kinds of puffer fish contain a poison that can be deadly for humans. Surprisingly, however, the fish are considered a special treat in some countries, especially Japan. In these places, skilled chefs know how to remove the poisonous parts of the fish before serving them.

The pill bug is a tiny creature that, like the three-banded armadillo, has a hard covering that it can roll up. The pill bug uses its special power to protect itself from the bites of lizards, frogs, and other predators.

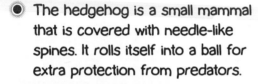

Pill bug

Pill bug rolled up

The hedgehog is a small mammal that is covered with needle-like spines. It rolls itself into a ball for extra protection from predators.

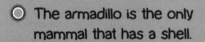

The armadillo is the only mammal that has a shell.

Hedgehog

Glossary

armor (AR-mur) a protective covering

bird droppings (BURD DROP-ings) the solid waste that comes out of a bird's body

disguise (diss-GYEZ) something that changes the way one looks so that one cannot be recognized

frill (FRIL) a ruffle or similar item used as decoration

larva (LAR-vuh) the worm-like form of many kinds of young insects

mammal (MAM-uhl) a warm-blooded animal that has a backbone, hair or fur on its skin, and drinks its mother's milk as a baby

mimic (MIM-ik) one who copies or imitates the look, sound, or behavior of other things

octopus (OK-tuh-puhss) a sea animal that has eight arms with suckers, three hearts, and a soft body

poisonous (POI-zuhn-uhss) containing a substance that can harm or kill a living thing when eaten

predators (PRED-uh-turs) animals that hunt and kill other animals for food

reptile (REP-tile) a cold-blooded animal, such as a snake, lizard, crocodile, or turtle, that has scaly skin, a backbone, and lungs

spikes (SPYEKS) sharp points

squid (SKWID) a long, soft-bodied sea animal with eight arms, two tentacles, and three hearts

tentacles (TEN-tuh-kuhlz) long, arm-like body parts used by some animals, such as squid, for catching prey

transform (trans-FORM) to change

unfurls (un-FURLZ) opens something that was wrapped or curled up

webbing (WEB-ing) skin that connects toes, arms, or other parts of an animal's body

Index

Bibliography

Courage, Katherine. "Unusual Offshore Octopods: The Weapon-Wielding Blanket Octopus." *Scientific American*. April 5, 2013. (http://blogs.scientificamerican.com/octopus-chronicles/2013/04/05/unusual-offshore-octopods-the-weapon-wielding-blanket-octopus-video/)

Forbes, Peter. *Dazzled and Deceived: Mimicry and Camouflage*. New Haven, CT: Yale University Press (2009).

Hansford, Dave. "Cuttlefish Change Color, Shape-Shift to Elude Predators." *National Geographic News*. August 6, 2008. (http://news.nationalgeographic.com/news/2008/08/080608-cuttlefish-camouflage-missions.html)

Wolfe, Art. *Vanishing Act*. New York: Bulfinch Press (2005).

Zimmer, Carl. "How the Pufferfish Got Its Puff." *Discover*. September 1, 1997. (http://discovermagazine.com/1997/sep/howthepufferfish1226#.UbDyIRyKfR2)

Read More

Smith, Molly. *Roly-Poly Pillbugs (No Backbone! The World of Invertebrates)*. New York: Bearport (2009).

Spirn, Michelle. *Octopuses (Smart Animals!)*. New York: Bearport (2007).

Yaw, Valerie. *Color-Changing Animals (Animals with Super Powers)*. New York: Bearport (2011).

Learn More Online

To learn more about shape-shifting animals, visit
www.bearportpublishing.com/AnimalswithSuperPowers

About the Author

Natalie Lunis has written many science and nature books for children.
She lives in the Hudson River Valley, just north of New York City.